AN EYE ON HONG KONG

Dragon Dancers

2001

Among the Chinese, the dragon is a symbol of luck and auspiciousness. He is a fantasy animal representing all that is good and brave. The ancients believed that he could control the weather and eliminate diseases and disasters and people hoped that the dragon would bless and protect them. Nowadays the dances are performed mostly at ceremonies, occasions when foreign dignitaries visit and at the Chinese Lunar New Year parade. The dance is performed by a long chain of men and can be of 9 up to 24 sections. This photograph was taken at a deliberately slow speed so as to emphasise the colour and movement of this splendid dance.

PREVIOUS PAGE
The Harbour

2000

Hong Kong's best-known panorama, from Lugard Road on the Peak, encompasses (in the foreground from left to right) Central, Wanchai and Causeway Bay on Hong Kong Island, and (in the distance) Kowloon on the north side of Victoria Harbour, Hong Kong's greatest asset has always been its magnificent natural sheltered harbour, now home to one of the world's busiest container ports and visited by over 175,000 ocean-going vessels a year. For over a hundred years, land reclamation has been slowly encroaching on the harbour, bringing the waterfronts of Tsim Sha Tsui and the island's north shore closer together. Today, almost every building on the island's north shore is on reclaimed land, and the ever-quickening pace of reclamation is giving some environmentalists and almost all the population of Hong Kong cause for extreme concern.

OVERLEAF
Causeway Bay Typhoon Shelter

1999

A stunning August sunset provides the backdrop to Central, North Wanchai and the Causeway Bay Typhoon Shelter. The Island Eastern Corridor snakes along the shoreline, and the office blocks of North Wanchai sparkle with extraordinary reflections. The craft moored in the shelter are a mix of two extremes: the expensive yachts owned by members of the Royal Hong Kong Yacht Club contrasting with the small sampans and working fishing boats which base themselves in the typhoon shelter. The new Hong Kong Convention and Exhibition Centre is in the right centre.

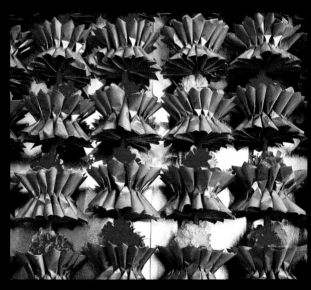

Sha Tin Races, Ladies' Day
1996

The public stands are packed to capacity. Without doubt horse racing is Hong Kong's most popular sport, mainly because it is the only legal form of gambling here. The Hong Kong Jockey Club was founded in 1884 but professional racing was not introduced until 1971. In the 1995/6 season the betting turnover was a staggering HK$80.7 billion of which 81% was paid back to punters in dividends, 12.8% in duty and HK$1.1 billion was donated to charity and sports organizations.

PREVIOUS PAGE
The Island
2000

Taken from the new "Waterfront" apartment complex above the Kowloon station for the airport this spectacular sunset view of the North shore of the Island on a steamy August evening stretches from North Wanchai in the left distance over to the Peak and Western district on the right. In the left foreground one can see the end of the Ocean Terminal in Tsimshatsui and the China Ferry Terminal before this.

INSIDE GATEFOLD
Festivals

A colourful collection of photographs taken at various festivals around Hong Kong. These show that behind the glittering modern high rise city there exists, parallel to it, an ancient culture which is very much alive and vibrant.

OVERLEAF
Lamma Island
1990

Sunset over Lamma Island from Headland Road. This view has remained unchanged for 25 years with just two notable exceptions: on the right is Ocean Park's rollercoaster, just one of the excitements offered by the 160-acre marine park which opened in 1977; and on Lamma Island an electric power station, with its prominent smoke stacks, which was built in 1980.

AN EYE ON HONG KONG

A Portfolio of Photographs
1970 – 2001
by Keith Macgregor

Foreword by Anthony Lawrence

Published by Pacific Century Publishers Ltd.

First published in Hong Kong in 1997 by Cameraman Ltd.
2nd edition published in 1998 by Pacific Century Publishers Ltd.
3rd edition published in 2000 by Pacific Century Publishers Ltd.
This edition published in 2002 by Pacific Century Publishers Ltd.

All enquiries to:
Pacific Century Publishers Ltd.
1603-4 Hon Kwok Jordan Centre, 7 Hillwood Road, Tsimshatsui, Kowloon, Hong Kong
Tel: 2376 2085   Fax: 2376 2137   e-mail: pacman@pacificcentury.com.hk

For enquiries regarding rights and terms to use photographs in this book and
Keith Macgregor's extensive photographic library please contact either the above or
access our website at: http://www.**photos**hongkong.com

All photography by Keith Macgregor©
Picture Editing by Magnus Bartlett & Keith Macgregor
Production & printing supervision by Twin Age Ltd.
Captions by Jill Trew
Jacket & book design by Margaret Ng

Printed in China

THIS BOOK IS DEDICATED TO:

Lindsay, my wife of 30 years;
Hugo, Lucy and Sophie, my children; Oscar, my grandson.
Jack and Dorothy Macgregor, my grandparents;
Robin and Midge Macgregor, my parents; Joanna Macgregor, my sister.
All my old staff of Banyan Tree; those who have been with me in
Cameraman Ltd and Pacific Century Publishers Ltd.
The people of Hong Kong.

Star Ferry

1989

A Star Ferry chases a vehicular ferry bound for Hung Hom in Victoria
Harbour. Photographed from the Peak with a long lens, the two ferries are
moving through a spectacular beam of light emanating from the massive
golden buildings at the China Ferry Terminal in Yau Ma Tei.

FOREWORD

BY ANTHONY LAWRENCE

B eauty, said the writer Lew Wallace, is in the eye of the beholder; but he wrote before the days of the modern camera. For the artist–photographer work begins not with just seeing, but with years of knowing, – an intense accumulated knowledge of land, sea and people.

This is the kind of experience which enables Keith Macgregor to be familiar with the exact moment when the dying sun, pausing along the crest of the hills, deepens the waters of the Hong Kong Harbour with a darker gold; or when the lights come on and all the streets and building at once seem to be celebrating some great birthday.

LEFT & ABOVE
Chek Lap Kok
1970 & 2000

Mainland junks floating on a becalmed sea near to Chek Lap Kok, now the site of the new airport. These delicate,butterfly-like sailing craft were in fact working engineless cargo boats which carried building materials, timber and other goods down the coast from Shantou & Xiamen (more usually known as Swatow and Amoy) and up the coast to Guangzhou (Canton). Junks were common here in the 70's but have now, sadly,all but disappeared. The above photograph shows the entrance to the Terminal building, which is the biggest covered structure in the world and was designed by Lord Norman Foster. Costing US$20 billion and only 9 years in construction, the new airport was the largest infrastructure project ever undertaken gobally.

His book denies any attempt at political analysis or local history - that ground has already been explored by many others. Instead he has drawn on 30 years of photographing the territory "to present an essay on its beauty, its colours and texture, and its local culture".

You might call it a work of Impressionism. Within the framework of a tour leading from Hong Kong Island across the Harbour to Kowloon and into the Northern New Territories and Outlying Islands. it is also a journey through time as well as space, with revealing portraits not only of Chinese faces but of ships, junks, festivals, ceremonies, great modern buildings, ancient villages.

For a western news correspondent like myself, the book has a special value. Like many other new arrivals expecting to stay only three years at most, I tried in haste to see and learn everything I could, as soon as possible. But in those far-off days of the 1960s I was working for the BBC as their correspondent for the whole of the Far East. Which meant that I was frequently away in Vietnam, or Indonesia, or any other area undergoing chaos or revolt. This went on for years. I would return from some uncomfortable trip to find the heart of Central undergoing profound changes. What a place of transition and expansion was this Hong Kong! I remember asking former Governor Sir (then) Murray Maclehose, why had they pulled down and replaced the attractive old Hong Kong Club building? He said he had consulted the local Chinese top brass and that was what they wanted.

It seemed in those years that every time I left Hong Kong, I returned to find a new road cutting through old tenements, a new skyscraper dominating the business area. A fascinating time, this feverish development of the Hong Kong quick-rich arena, transformed sometimes by visionaries hiring world-leading architects, sometimes by men simply out to exploit for cash every single cubic foot of the land they had bought.

Central Hong Kong had spread so fast that parts of the Harbour area were unrecognisable. Inevitable of course when the population of a 1,000 square kilometre territory doubles from three to six million or more. What has made Hong Kong such a fascinating challenge for the western reporter is the variety of the place - not only the changes but also the places that time has failed to erode. Those villages I visited in the first six months since

Kowloon-Canton Railway Terminal

1976

Completed in 1915, the station was the terminus for Hong Kong's rail link with the interior of China. From the 1930s this was connected to the Trans-Siberian Railway, allowing those who wished to avoid the six-week steamer trip from Hong Kong to England to reach Victoria station in London just 18 days from Hong Kong. The station was demolished in 1978. Behind the station are the YMCA, the Peninsula and Sheraton Hotels.

my arrival, what has happened to them? Some have vanished to make way for New Towns housing each a quarter of a million; but others remain unchanged from centuries ago.

Surprises await today's newcomers. They will look almost in vain for ricefields. The great tattered sails of cargo junks are gone from the harbour, the work done by containers now. But Hong Kong Chinese are a practical lot. You might have expected that by now steel scaffolding would have taken over the building scene from the traditional bamboo; yet bamboo is still very widely used, even in erecting the most modern gems of architecture. Bamboo poles are cheap and easy to fix, they can be clamped to higher storeys without support on the pavement below, and rise to any height. Scaffolding is no work for the heavyweight but Cantonese men are well suited to it, being wiry, slight of build and quick in their reactions.

Macgregor's "Then and Now" juxta-position of pictures brings all these contrasts vividly alive. For me they recall the past, including my first visit, accompanied, to Chinese Opera - "He's carrying a whip, that means he's on horse-back". I see the junks moving regally through the Harbour (vanished now). Free from today's pollution-haze I see from the Peak the great vista reaching to the high hills of the New Territories; and (still part of today's Hong Kong) I am able to see again as I did years ago the dragon races at Tai O and stroll again through the street markets of Kowloon and Stanley.

An abiding impression of this "portfolio of photographs" is the human landscape - Chinese faces, street-scenes and encounters. They reveal more about the Hong Kong Chinese than much of what psychological and cultural experts write. They show the energy of people, their feelings for the family, their general cheerfulness. A pleasing ingredient, this, to the visual pleasures of "An Eye on Hong Kong".

Lai Chi Wo Village

1997

This almost perfectly preserved walled village lies on the west side of
Crooked Harbour (Kat O Hoi) in the North East part of the New Territories,
on the border of the Special Administrative Region with China.

Wanchai

1995

It seems extraordinary that, despite new construction techniques, the use of traditional bamboo scaffolding is still standard practice in Hong Kong. The unsung heroes of the construction industry who create these vast, apparently flimsy frames seem oblivious to danger as they sit, often without harnesses, as high as 60 storeys up a building, lashing together the poles. One recent statistic claims that some three million pieces of bamboo are tied together around newly constructed, or disappearing buildings every year in Hong Kong.

CONTENTS

Foreword   23

Introduction   30

Hong Kong Island   50

Kowloon   110

New Territories   138

Outlying Islands   190

Index   226

Technical Background   227

Hei Ling Chau

1973

Pulling in the nets at Hei Ling Chau, a small island
which lies to the southeast of Lantau. Fishing is very
much a family affair in Hong Kong and every
member of the family, old and young, is involved.

INTRODUCTION

Macgregor House, Shanghai
....
1998

Caldbeck Macgregor's offices at 44 Foochow road, built in 1937
to replace the original 1894 building known as "the Auld Hoose".
The Elizabethan style building was somewhat on the lines of an
old English inn with a large interior courtyard and a handsome
gabled and oak panelled hall, which was used for meetings or as
a reception room. It had a very fine wine cellar carefully constructed to allow the greatest care and attention to be given to
the company's stocks. The architects were Palmer &Turner. It was
seized by the new government in 1949 and has been declared a
protected building, hence it's longevity.

My great-grandfather John Macgregor was the younger son of a Scottish crofter family in Callander, Central Scotland, and was forced, because of the primogeniture inheritance laws in Scotland, to seek his fortune elsewhere. He joined the merchant navy in Glasgow and headed East to China. After a few voyages there he set up in business for himself, going into the wine and spirits trade in 1864, the same year which saw the foundation of the Hongkong and Shanghai Banking Corporation. These were turbulent times in China with the Ching dynasty in its death throes and foreigners still experiencing the aftermath of the Taiping rebellion. However the Suez Canal opened in 1869 and the telegraph reached Hong Kong and Shanghai in 1870 which gave a huge boost to China Coast traders. John Macgregor remained in Shanghai but branches of Caldbeck Macgregor and Co. Ltd., as the company was then known, opened in Hong Kong, Tien Tsin, Penang, Kuala Lumpur and Ipoh. He was an avid horse racing enthusiast and built up a large stable which he raced all over China, usually riding his horses himself. He retired to Kent in the 1890s leaving the business to his sons, Norman and Jack,

my grandfather, who took over the firm at the very young age of 25. He moved to Hong Kong and met Dorothy Shelton Hooper who was born in Hong Kong and was the daughter of the first manager of Sir Paul Chater's Hong Kong Land Investment Company. They were married in St John's Cathedral in 1911, where I was also married exactly 60 years later. My father, Robin was born in 1916 just before my grandfather was gassed in Normandy while serving as an officer on the Somme in the Great War. He survived and after a year in a German prisoner of war camp returned to Hong Kong to resume running the firm, which involved moving back and forth between Hong Kong and Shanghai. He also travelled to London from Hong Kong many times on the Trans-Siberian railway to visit his wife and sons who were at schools in England.

My mother, Imogen Newman, was born in Shanghai. Her father was a solicitor and her mother a leading light in Shanghai

PREVIOUS PAGE
Hong Kong from Glenealy

1879

The exquisite pencil and watercolour is by Constance Gordon Cumming (1837-1924). She arrived in Hong Kong on Christmas Day 1878 and her subsequent experiences in the East are described in her book "Wanderings in China". This was painted at Glenealy, the property of the mercantile house of Gibb Livingstone and Co.

(courtesy of Martyn Gregory © and the collection of Mr. and Mrs. Peter Thompson of Hong Kong)

1948

amateur dramatic life. She and her elder sister Marylou were two very pretty young ladies and were in great demand in the vibrant and hectic pre-war social life of Shanghai. My father met her in 1938 and they became engaged in 1940 when my mother was only 18. In 1941, as war had broken out with Germany my father went to Calcutta to enlist in the British army. My mother followed three months later and on the stopover in Hong Kong was joined by my grandparents who then sailed with her to Calcutta for the wedding. Fortunately my grandmother did not travel light as while the wedding was taking place in Calcutta both Shanghai and Hong Kong fell to the Japanese. Their war was consequently spent in India in relative comfort compared with the rest of their family members who were not so fortunate and were incarcerated in various Japanese prisoner of war camps.

I was born in Bangalore in 1946. Six months later I landed in Hong Kong from a troop ship in the arms of my mother.

The Harbour and City

1948

This photograph was taken by Mee Cheung of Ice House Street from May Road. It shows clearly the Hong Kong and Shanghai Bank, the cricket ground and the naval dockyard. Government House is with its newly acquired tower, courtesy of General Isogai, the Japanese governor during the occupation.

2000

1970

The Harbour

2000

The phenomenal changes since 1970 are obvious. Hong Kong has grown into a sophisticated international city with architecture to rival anywhere in the world. Across the harbour in Kowloon is where the greatest changes are now taking place. One can already seen the large reclamation project of Yau Ma Tei (centre left) and now that the airport is at Chek Lap Kok all height restrictions on the Kowloon peninsula have been removed.

PREVIOUS PAGES

The Harbour and the City

1970 & 2000

These two spectacular panoramas were taken from almost exactly the same spot at the end of Pollock's Path on the Peak. This view has acted as a yardstick for tracing Hong Kong's rapid development over this period. They both cover the whole harbour, the North shore of Hong Kong island and Kowloon with the New Territories beyond; but what a difference 30 years has made! In the earlier photograph the Furama Hotel is in the middle of construction. It was to be the tallest building until the Connaught Centre in 1973 (see page 43). The Hong Kong Hilton and the Mandarin Hotel were already open but Wanchai and Causeway Bay were very thinly developed. In the later picture the new Tsing Ma bridge to the airport is just visible on the far left. The shape of the harbour is just recognisable but for how long? The viewpoint of both photographs was the site of the Chief Justice's house which was destroyed in the Second World War and was rumoured to be haunted. It was finally very badly redeveloped in the late 80's.

If I had been old enough to use a camera then I would have recorded a small city in disarray trying to pick itself up after a cruel Japanese occupation which had forced half of the pre-war population back to China. The city was in a sorry state and very short of food and fuel. Even the Peninsula Hotel was an army barracks. My grandfather's house on Barker Road was a ruin with most of its woodwork stripped to provide fuel for the desperate people of Hong Kong during the occupation. But it was not long before these same people were back on their feet again. However on the mainland things were much worse. China was in the midst of a devastating civil war following straight after the horrors of the Japanese invasion. Hong Kong was about to experience the consequences of this in the form of a huge influx of refugees both immediately after the war and more so after 1949.

Like many other British and Chinese businessmen my grandfather's over-riding concern was to rebuild his shattered and bankrupted business. He did this remarkably quickly with the help of the Hongkong and Shanghai Bank. He even opened a branch in Tokyo in 1947. My father was sent to Kuala Lumpur to reopen the business there but in 1948 with things not looking too hopeful for western companies in China a decision was made to expand, not in Asia but into Africa. With hindsight this was, of course, unfortunate as Asia was and is the place to be. It did mean, however, that we spent ten happy years in beautiful Kenya.

On returning to Hong Kong to live in 1959 we found a very different place: a population which had grown from 1.5 million in 1947 to 3 million, a virtually autonomous territory administratively and financially and a powerful Chinese élite on equal terms with British merchants in all spheres of public life.

An economic miracle was taking place with Hong Kong now a manufacturer of textiles, plastics and later, consumer electronics.

A butterfly of the South China Sea

1971

This magnificent example of a working mainland sailing junk was photographed in the Llama Channel off Aberdeen. This was a wonderful place to capture such images and I used to lie in wait on my mother's boat waiting for the junks to pass by on their way from Amoy and Swatow to Canton and beyond.
They are sadly missed.

Convention and Exhibition Centre and Cheung Kong Centre

2000

The new extension to the Convention and Exhibition Centre is clearly visible in this
dusk view from the Peak. The complex, costing $4.8 Billion was the venue of the official
handover ceremony marking the end of 156 years of British colonial rule. It was
designed by Wong and Ouyang of Hong Kong and Skidmore, Owings and Merrill
of Chicago. The new hi-tech Cheung Kong Centre, next to the Bank of China,
is the latest addition to Hong Kong's skyscrapers.

Lantau Flowers

1997

Let us hope that we will continue to be able to see scenes
like this in Lantau now that the airport road link has opened
up the island to massive potential development.

RIGHT

The Lantau Link, Tsing Ma Bridge

2000

This bridge is the key element in the 34 kilometre
direct road and rail network leading to Hong Kong
International Airport at Chek Lap Kok.
At 2.2 km the bridge will be the world's longest
combined road and rail suspension bridge.
The main span is a staggering 1,377 metres
and the total length of the 160,000 km suspension
cable wire is enough to circle the world four times.
The new airport opened on July 6, 1998.

Tap Mun Island Ta Chiu Festival

1999

This festival happens every 10 years and old residents and family members
return to this tiny island in Mirs Bay from all over the world to join in
the unique 5 day event. Here village elders and guests are taking the God
Tien Hau to a waiting boat for the start of a tour to a neighbouring
island. One of the most fascinating things about Hong Kong is that, despite
the huge outward changes since the photograph on the right was taken, old
Chinese local customs and traditions like this are as strong as ever.

RIGHT
Central and the Peak

1974

Photographed from above Mt. Nicholson in a helicopter, this view of
Central and the Peak shows Connaught Centre (now Jardine House) as the tallest
building in the city. The cricket pitch can be seen clearly in front.

My own memories of it are limited as I was only here for eight weeks a year, two years out of three. In this short time away from school in England I was much too preoccupied with the normal pursuits of the average expatriate teenager: girls, beaches, parties and watersports. If I had had then my present interests I would have photographed a city which still had many of its grand Victorian buildings, a New Territories where age-old methods of farming and village life remained untouched by the rapid changes occurring in the urban areas. Sha Tin for example was still a verdant valley of rice paddies and Sai Kung looked little different from remote areas of China.

On my 21st birthday my parents gave me my first serious camera. From that day, unknown to me, my life was set. After leaving Oxford University, I joined a bus going overland from London to Kathmandu in Nepal. Armed with the new camera, a few rolls of film, sleeping bag and £120 in traveller's cheques I set off to India in a totally inadequate vehicle (it broke down 6 times before reaching Teheran!). It was on this trip that the seeds of my passion for travel photography were sown. After crossing the Bosphorus into Asia it required very strong discipline not to use all of my meagre supply of film in the first few days.

The journey lasted three months and ended with me in hospital in Hong Kong laid up with severe amoebic hepatitis. After a slow recovery my long-suffering parents, who had been dead against the bus trip in the first place, felt that I needed to learn about life and earn my own living, so I was dispatched off to New York where I joined J.E. Seagram as a management trainee. It was there that I learnt to print my own negatives in the cramped confines of my minuscule West Slide apartment. This must be the moment when many photographers become truly hooked. I look back at both the results of my photographic efforts on the bus trip and my early attempts at print making with some amusement but the wonder of that first print remains locked in my memory.

My father's untimely death in 1969 brought me unexpectedly back to Hong Kong. I had had no plans prior to this of

Happy Valley

1975 & 1994

As this was the only piece of flat land on the island it was chosen to be the site of the racecourse. Known in Chinese as Wong Nei Chong or "Yellow mud stream", it was a noxious, unhealthy place full of swamps and rice fields. It was drained in 1844 and the first race meeting was on December 17, 1846. The racecourse is still there, but what a far cry from those days! These two photographs show the huge developments which took place in a mere 19 years.

living here but my brief encounter with corporate life in New York had convinced me that it should be avoided at all costs. Photography as a profession had not even occurred to me. It was only when I accompanied my mother to Angkor Wat in Cambodia in 1970 that I considered it seriously. I was carried away by the powerful beauty of that fascinating ancient city buried in the jungle and I was also inspired there by the courteous and unselfish encouragement and help given to me by Bela Kalman, a Hungarian American photographer I met there. In Hong Kong our next door neighbour was the renowned Time Life photographer, Larry Burrows who also inspired and urged me to go ahead. His death later in Cambodia was a tragic loss to all who knew him.

I began by photographing children and families. This is an excellent discipline for a new boy in the profession and gave me the chance to learn to be a good printmaker and at the same time earn a very reasonable living. I was then ventured into corporate and advertising, industrial and aerial photography and most importantly some travel assignments.
I also began photographing Hong Kong whenever I had the time.

香港 　　HONG KONG 　　Close Call

In 1974 a leading hotel agreed to sponsor an exhibition of my photographs of Hong Kong and Indonesia and the consequence of this was the birth of Cameraman and the Hong Kong calendar business, which continues to this day.

Some years later I was persuaded by friends to try and do something to upgrade the very poor standard of postcards in Hong Kong. After a slow start this took off and it now gives me a huge amount of satisfaction to know that every year almost two million people all over the world receive one of my postcards through their letter boxes.

I gradually ceased to do corporate and advertising work in the early '80s as a result of an increasing involvement in Nic Nac Limited (later renamed Banyan Tree), a business with my wife Lindsay, which dealt in Asian art, antiques, carpets, furniture and anything interesting and beautiful which we could find on our travels. The rapid growth of this made it difficult to do much else but the calendars and postcards on the photographic side.

This book is a result of 30 years of searching the length and breadth of Hong Kong for the types of photograph that suit those mediums. It has been an exhilarating task in a place which never

A city in constant movement

1978 & 1998

On the left is Tai Yuen street , Wanchai, where hawkers sell everything from fruit and vegetables to T-shirts, nightdresses, haberdashery and hardware. It is actually a thoroughfare and every time a vehicle appears the whole market has to move aside. The postcard pictured above was taken from a street in Kowloon City, where it was possible to create the illusion of the planes colliding with the rooftops. This was one of the last Jumbos to land at Kaitak airport.

ceases to surprise and fascinate. Editing the thousands of photographs has been an extraordinary undertaking but once a theme had been established, that of a journey round the whole territory from Central to the border with China, it became much easier. Sifting through all the early photographs has opened up a flood of memories. For example, the shot of the cricket ground in Chater Road reminds me of the wonderful afternoons spent there as a schoolboy. I can still feel the butterflies in my stomach as I charged in to bowl against the local Hong Kong schoolboy cricket team. Those of the Hong Kong Club take me back to the all too few times I was taken there to lunch by my grandfather and father as a young lad. The views from our flat in Headland Road (pages 90 and 91) are particularly poignant because this is where I lived from 1959 till when I was married in 1971 and where I returned to live from 1989 to 1992. To start and finish up one's life in Hong Kong with a view like this, which has hardly changed in the intervening years, is remarkable considering the enormous changes which have taken place everywhere else. I am truly fortunate.

Hong Kong is a place whose people I have grown to love and respect, whose rhythms and colours intoxicate. It is also a place which sometimes bewilders and frustrates. Like most long-term residents here I suspect that we continually wish to escape from it but within weeks or days we hunger to return. The moment when the aeroplane touched down at Kai Tak and now at Chek Lap Kok one is carried away by a feeling of excitement and anticipation. Hong Kong is truly alive and this above all is what must be preserved in the future which lies ahead. Although I now live in London, I hope to return again and again to continue to record the life and times of this remarkable city to which I owe so much. This is my tribute to Hong Kong and its hard-working wonderful people. Long may it and they continue to prosper and flourish.

Old Hong Kong Club building

1978

The elegant colonnaded Hong Kong Club, which was founded in 1844 and moved here in 1897, was demolished in 1981 to make way for a high-rise building, which houses the club in a spacious, modern setting, and also yields substantial rental income from the many floors of offices above. Nonetheless, there are still those in Hong Kong who regret the demise of Central's last remaining example of Victorian colonial architecture. In the foreground early risers practise tai-chi, the traditional Chinese slow-motion form of callisthenics. Early in the morning one can see men and women of all ages throughout Hong Kong working through a series of movements with almost balletic grace.

The Hong Kong Cricket Club

1975

Just before the club moved to the wider open spaces of Wong Nei Chong Gap in June 1975. Surprisingly, given the pace of change in this part of town, the three blocks overlooking the ground are still standing in 2000 on the left is the old Bank of China Building; in the centre is Prince's Building, an office and shopping block ; on the right is the Mandarin Hotel, built by the Hong Kong Land Company in 1963, and since then consistently listed amongst the world's best hotels.

THE ISLAND

Central
1996

From the roof of the YMCA in Kowloon in dramatic early morning light which highlights the Hongkong and Shanghai Bank on the left, Jardine House in the centre and the towers of Exchange Square to the right. On the Peak the silhouette of the new Peak Tower building, completed in 1996, can be seen. The Clock Tower, built in 1916, provides an interesting architectural contrast in the foreground.

RIGHT
Central
2000

This shot of the glittering lights of Central was taken with a 60-second exposure from the carpark of the Ocean Terminal. The view encompasses the stunning outlines of I.M.Pei's Bank of China across to "The Center" on the edge of Western District. To the right of the Bank of China is Cheung Kong's new flagship building "Cheung Kong Centre" which is probably the most hi-tech building in Asia.

PREVIOUS PAGE
The south side of the Island

This view from the Matilda Hospital on Mount Kellett Road encompasses, from right to left, the fishing port of Aberdeen with the island of Ap Lei Chau, Shum Wan, Wong Chuk Hang, Shouson Hill and on to Deep Water Bay, Repulse Bay and in the far distance the Stanley Peninsula. Lamma Island is on the far right of the picture.

Kennedy Town

1977

A typical old building in Eastern Street, Kennedy Town. Almost all these low-rise balconied blocks have been replaced by highrise constructions.

LEFT

Central

2000

This view of Hong Kong island's Central district and the Peak, taken from the Tsimshatsui Clock Tower promenade stretches from Pacific Place on the far left to the edges of Western district on the right. The two tallest buildings are the Bank of China, left, and "the Center" on the right. At night the latter's lights change their colours continually. The very white building in the centre is Jardine House (formerly Connaught Centre) and on it's right is Exchange Square in which are housed most of the region's international merchant banks.

Central

1972 & 1995

The view from the old Hong Kong Club, across to the Supreme Court building. Opened in 1912 by the Governor, Sir Frederick Lugard, the granite building boasts Ionic columns, balustrades and arches reminiscent of late Victorian architecture in Britain. The building was designed by Webb and Bell who were also architects of the facade of Buckingham Palace. The Supreme Court moved out in 1983, when it became the home of the Legislative Council. Beyond it is the old China Bank building, which served for many years as a control centre for China's financial affairs in Hong Kong, and also for Beijing's political and diplomatic activities. To its right is the old Hongkong and Shanghai Bank building, built in the 1930s and demolished to make way for Norman Foster's new building in 1985. Further right is the Standard Chartered Bank building. On the far left is the Hong Kong Hilton, and in the foreground the Hong Kong Cricket Club - all of which have now gone. On page 57 is The Legislative Council building, now dwarfed by the new Hong Kong and Shanghai Bank.

Douglas Castle

1995

Now called University Hall, in an eerie light that emphasized the building's neo-gothic
features. Built in 1861 on a hill in Pokfulam by a Hong Kong shipping magnate,
John Douglas Lapraic, the odd mix of gothic and colonial styles, with turrets, battlements
and colonial arched balconies is strangely imposing. It was sold to the Société des
Missions Etrangères de Paris in 1894, who renamed it Nazareth House.
The French monks added a chapel and crypt, and stayed there until 1954 when it
was sold to the University of Hong Kong and became a student hall of residence.

LEFT
The old Post Office

1977

Opened in 1912 but sadly demolished in 1978 to make way for an undistinguished
commercial building called World Wide House.

The Bank of China, Cheung Kong Centre and HSBC

2000

Designed by brilliant Chinese American architect I.M.Pei, and completed in 1987, the 70-storey building stands at night like an almost transparent gossamer wing of a butterfly. With its series of dramatic triangular prisms, topped by twin masts, the building forcefully creates the commanding impact that the Bank of China required from its chosen architect.

The Cheung Kong Centre, built in 1999, was designed by Leo A. Daly & Associates. It is the most hi-tech building in Hong Kong with a design very much influenced by strict "feng shui" requirements. At night it is particularly prominent and the lighting can be adjusted by computer to almost any colour and configuration. The renowned merchant bank, Goldman Sachs, has leased a number of the higher floors.

On its right is the headquarters of HSBC, built in 1985 to Lord Norman Foster's unique design, and supposedly the most expensive single building ever built.

RIGHT
Lippo Centre

Taken from a small observation tower in the middle of Hong Kong Park, this shot shows some of Hong Kong's best architecture against a sky of pastel blues and pinks. Citibank Tower is to the left, with the lower floors of the Bank of China next to it, and the Lippo Centre (formerly the Bond Centre) dominating on the right. Designed by eminent American architect Paul Rudolph, and opened in 1988, the light from the many facets of the Centre's two hexagonal towers provides particular visual interest.

Victoria Harbour
2000

Victoria Harbour from Lugard Road, the
narrow road circling the Peak, offering a
different, but equally magnificent view
every few yards. Pictures from up here
need updating twice a year because land
reclamation and the pace of building
make the scene change so rapidly. This is
rightly considered to be one of the most
exciting night views in the world.

Novice ballet dancers
1990

Novice ballet dancers at Jean Wong's School of Ballet. Ms Wong's school, the best known in the territory, has produced some fine international stars including dancers for London's Royal Ballet Company.

LEFT
Smiling Faces

The casual visitor to Hong Kong whose only experience of its people might be of the shopkeepers and taxi drivers of Tsim Sha Tsui could easily be misled into believing that it is an unfriendly and aggressive place. This is far from the truth; with a little effort and understanding he will find a genuine and friendly response and many a warm smile will greet him.

Harbour fishing

1980

Fishing outside the Royal Hong Kong Yacht Club. Even in those days the
harbour did not appear to be the cleanest of places and one has to wonder
about the condition of the catch from these waters. This might explain why a
scene like this would be very rare today.

LEFT
Western Harbour

1993

A cruise liner glides through shimmering water at sunset, having just left the Ocean Terminal on the right, and the western harbour is dotted with ships waiting to load or unload their goods.

PAGE 66
Central from Pacific Place

1990

This staggering sunset appeared quite unexpectedly. No filters were used. The shot captures the Bank of China and several other buildings at an unusual angle. The Hilton's floodlit rooftop tennis court is clearly visible on the left. The hotel has since been demolished, making way for the new Cheung Kong Centre, which will yield even greater profits for its owners than the Hilton did.

Chinese Opera

Opera performances in specially erected 'matshed' theatres are often an integral part of local festivals. Traditional Cantonese opera is very much alive in Hong Kong, enjoyed by the younger generation as well as by their parents and grandparents. It depends heavily on colour and theatrical effects for its impact. Traditionally, scenery was not used beyond a plain wooden chair or table, everything else was supplied by the imagination. These days more realistic sets are common, but the performer still dominates the stage. Actors specialize in certain roles, which they continue to play throughout their careers. Singing is done in a characteristic falsetto voice that takes many years to perfect. Although it may sound harsh, it can still be highly expressive. In the past only men could become actors, but today all roles are unisex, depending on the talent of the individual. There are some 500 professional singers, actors and acrobats working in the profession augmented by visiting troupes from different regions of China.

Showtime

1995

Pupils from Jean Wong's junior ballet school put on a New Year
performance at Tai Koo Plaza.

RIGHT
Causeway Bay & the Typhoon Shelter

1994

On the island this is the busiest and most popular place for shopping.
It hardly sleeps, with shops staying open late into the night. The entrance
to the Cross Harbour Tunnel is on the right; an average of 125,650 vehicles
cross the harbour through it every day. The new buildings of the reclaimed
Wanchai North are on the far right.

North Wanchai

2000

The Hong Kong Convention & Exhibition Centre opened in 1997 to host the main Handover ceremony. Designed by the Chicago firm of Skidmore, Owings & Merrill and a local firm, Wong & Ouyang, it cost HK$3.4 billion and has 28,000 square metres of exhibition space and a 4,500 seat conference hall. Central Plaza is on the right with Causeway Bay on the left. The daylight picture was taken on July 1st, the public holiday marking the Handover. A small flotilla of boats and helicopters passed through the harbour to celebrate this momentous occasion.

OVERLEAF & PAGES 78-79

Trams in Johnston Road, Wanchai

1984

Hong Kong's tram service began in 1904 and by 1912 double-decker cars were in use, although it was not until 1925 that the roofs were enclosed to protect passengers from scorching sun and heavy downpours. Today the trams continue to provide a fascinating and inexpensive, if rather slow, ride along 30 kilometres of Hong Kong's busiest roads. Over the years the traditional green colour of the trams has given way to the brilliant multi-coloured palate of advertisers. The first advertisements were displayed on small panels which were sold to individual advertisers, but more recently the whole body of a tram has been used as a promotional base for selling a myriad of items sought by the Hong Kong consumer - just about anything from computers and portable phones to ginseng, insect r epellent, or noodles. Standards of design and creativity are constantly improving, and today's trams are probably the largest, most inventive collection of moving billboards in the world.

Moon Festival

1992

Lanterns and flowers on sale in Lockhart Road in readiness for the Moon or Mid-Autumn Festival. Essential to the celebrations are paper lanterns, produced mainly in China, in an eclectic mix of traditional and modern designs that can feature anything from a Chinese lion or mythical horse to a jet or a gaudily-coloured tank. The proprietor in this picture adds to the charm of the scene by wearing traditional Chinese dress - a rare sight in Hong Kong these days.

Tiger Balm Gardens Pagoda

Built in 1935, funded by the wealthy Chinese philanthropist Aw Boon Haw who made his fortune out of Tiger Balm, a famous cure-all which relieves asthma, sore throats, insect bites and much else.

LEFT
Causeway Bay

2001

From Sir Cecil's Ride, a footpath winding round Mount Butler, said to be a favourite spot of the very able governor, Sir Cecil Clementi, who took up the post in 1925. He was an intellectual, spoke fluent Chinese and wrote poetry. He and his adored wife, Lady Penelope loved Hong Kong, and, on reluctantly leaving in 1930, said that "they would have stayed here rather than anywhere else in the world." Clearly the view from the path has completely changed since then, but it still offers an excellent vantage point and a fine walk.

Shau Kei Wan Typhoon Shelter

1994

Small sampans share this shelter with larger ocean-going fishing vessels. This particular
spot has since been filled in, and the boats have been moved further into the harbour.

RIGHT
Shau Kei Wan

1996

The bustle of the Kam Wa Street market is captured with a long lens and a slow speed.
This is where the tramway ends and the trams turn full circle and start their long journey
back to Kennedy Town, which is the western terminus of the system.

Wanchai Market

1980s

Chinese vegetables for sale in Wanchai Market. Hong
Kong's markets never cease to delight with their enticing
array of fresh fruit and vegetables and their boisterous
stall-holders. The tradition of buying food fresh each day is
deeply entrenched in the Hong Kong lifestyle, and markets
continue to hold their own in the war against convenience
shopping in supermarkets. Hong Kong people also
consume a massive quantity of oranges, often served
at the end of a meal.

FAR RIGHT
Ta Kwu Ling

1996

Harvesting vegetables in the closed area on the
border with China, across which workers come every day to
tend the high-quality produce in this area, replacing Hong
Kong's own farm labourers who have been attracted away
by better-paid work in other industries. The vegetables,
which are grown without heavy use of chemicals, command
a higher price than those imported from China, and go
straight to the tables of Hong Kong's top hotels.

Shek O

1996

Shek O Headland, taken from just under D'Aguilar Peak. It seems extraordinary to find
this magnificent, wild coastline and rough scrubby vegetation so near an urban centre.
The headland itself has changed little over the past quarter century, although more sand
has been added to Shek O Beach which is packed with sunbathers at weekends. Beyond is
the Tat Hong Channel, with the island of Tung Lung in the distance; the little island in the
foreground is Ng Fan Chau.

Shek O Golf and Country Club

1996

This exclusive private club has occupied one of the most beautiful corners of Hong Kong
for some seventy years.

Stanley Bay and the Market

1980 & 2001

Named after Lord Stanley, Secretary of State for the Colonies, this was an established village with some 2,000 inhabitants in 1841. A battery and fort were quickly established and, in the 1930's a new fort was built on the headland, with barracks, soldiers' and officers' quarters, a school, church and mess. The British army left in 1994 leaving the magnificent site for developers. Today, Stanley is predominantly a middle-class residential area, but somehow it has managed to keep something of a seaside village atmosphere, with its narrow streets and bustling and hugely popular market, parts of which are pictured above.

South Bay

1992 & 1976

This view over the bay and the Lamma Channel, supposedly one of the busiest shipping lanes in the world, has remained unchanged for years. The beach has been enlarged to increase the attraction of swimming here. It is a peaceful place although very popular in summer. The tranquil shot of two small sampans heading off to fish in the bay at dusk

Lido complex

1996

The gaudy but incredibly popular Lido complex, built by the Fung Ping Fan family, lies in front of the Life Guards Association on Repulse Bay Beach. Every morning, the Lido's concrete Buddhist garden, built in 1990, is flooded with visitors from Japan, Korea, Taiwan and Mainland China who come to photograph the Disneyland versions of figures from Chinese religion and mythology that ornament the site. On the previous page the three rams set against the sunset are messengers of the gods, while the goddess in the extravagantly-fringed head-dress is the sea goddess Tin Hau, the Queen of Heaven, and one of Hong Kong's most worshipped Taoist divinities. On this page is the serene figure of the Goddess of Mercy, Kwun Yum, who is loved and worshipped by Buddhists as well as Taoists.

PREVIOUS PAGE

Repulse Bay

1996

The sandy shallow bay got its name from the 19th-century pirate-chaser, HMS Repulse. Once a preferred picnic spot for the privileged, and accessible only by boat, it is now the easiest beach on the island to reach by public transport and tens of thousands flock here during the long hot months despite occasional scares about the cleanliness of the water. More sand was added in 1996 to increase beach capacity. Views from the expensive residential apartments behind the beach are spectacular - even by Hong Kong's high standards. The middle photograph on the right shows these apartments just before night falls.

The Repulse Bay Hotel

1978

This wonderful old hotel, which opened on New Year's Day in 1920, was best known for its gracious open verandah that looked across the bay, a favourite place for afternoon tea or dinner under twirling ceiling fans. The widespread public dismay when the hotel was torn down in 1982 for redevelopment led the owners, Hongkong and Shanghai Hotels, to incorporate a replica of the restaurant into the new complex, but inevitably the atmosphere is completely different.

Deep Water Bay and Lamma Island

2001

Taken from Repulse Bay Road this view shows Deep Water Bay and Lamma island
in the distance. The mansion in the foreground used to be the old Air Commodore's
residence and was the first private home in Hong Kong to sell for HK$ 1 million.
It is probably worth more than 200 times that figure today even after the Asian
economic downturn.

Fisherwoman

1986

Fisherwoman in a traditional Tanka hat, Aberdeen. These woven straw hats, with flattened crowns and turned down brims, are worn by both men and women in fishing communities throughout the region. They are made over the border in Guangdong Province.

LEFT

Sampan

1976

Sampan buzzing through Aberdeen Harbour. These small motorized boats still weave in and out of the larger vessels in the harbour, ferrying people and goods around, just as they did 20 years ago. The only change is in the style of the fishing boats behind - their traditional wooden junk-like hulls have been superseded by a sleeker and more efficient design.

RIGHT

Aberdeen

1984

Preparing wooden casks to hold fish landed from the boats. The boy chisels out Chinese characters in the wood, while his mother fills in the indented characters with red paint.

PREVIOUS PAGE

Deep Water Bay

1996

Luxury residential apartment blocks line Repulse Bay Road above the Bay. Island Road and its smaller houses and apartments hug the shoreline. Middle Island with its small yacht club is in the centre and through the gap one can see Repulse and South Bays with Headland Road above.

Aberdeen

1977

The busy fishing port with the island of Ap Lei Chau behind, seen from the air.
Ap Lei Chau has since undergone rapid development, and a large estate of
highrise public housing blocks now dominates the island's skyline. However,
the island's long-established boat building industry, visible in this picture, has
survived, and today wooden junks and other small craft are still being built
at the water's edge.

Aberdeen, Chinese New Year

1974

This large natural harbour has long been used by the Chinese. In the Ming Dynasty wood of the incense tree, which grew abundantly in Hong Kong, was shipped from here to Guangzhou. When the British arrived, the harbour was named after Lord Aberdeen, who was Foreign Secretary from 1841-1846. By 1860 it was chosen as the location for Hong Kong's first dock for ship repairs, with the Royal Navy its chief customer. Although its importance as a general port waned, the town continues to be a centre for commercial fishing and ship repairs.

Dragon Boat Races
1974

Aberdeen Harbour is one of the most exciting venues to watch Hong Kong's famous dragon boat races. The races are held throughout Hong Kong - as well as in Central and Southern China - to celebrate the Double Fifth (the fifth day of the fifth moon in the Chinese calendar). The long canoe-like boats, in which the paddlers sit two-abreast, are headed by magnificent dragon heads which are detached after the race and kept in local temples for the remainder of the year. The Chinese dragon is a beneficent creature, not the unpleasant character of European mythology, and has a wide mouth decorated with whiskers, and a beard which hides a shining pearl. The biggest dragon boats can be up to 100 feet long, with as many as 50 paddlers, a drummer who sets the pace, and an oarsman who stands at the stern and steers. It would be very difficult to take this shot today; the boats no longer race so closely together, and the races cover a longer distance.

Aberdeen, Chinese New Year

1996

At this time of year the majority of the fishing fleet returns home to celebrate the New Year with their families, now living in apartments rather than on their boats as they did in the past. As a result Aberdeen is jam packed and the sound of firecrackers is heard all over the harbour even though they are officially banned.

Aberdeen, Lamma Island and the South China Sea

2001

This view over the town and harbour of Aberdeen is from the Matilda Hospital on Mount Kellett on a very clear night in August. The tip of Stanley Peninsula can be seen on the far left and Lamma Island on the right. Aberdeen's bright lights are in the centre with the massed apartment buildings of Ap Li Chau across the now narrow stretch of water. It is quite a change from the small fishing village with a few low rise buildings, which we can see on page 102.

Aberdeen Harbour, Chinese New Year

1996

Aberdeen is home to Hong Kong's largest fishing fleet. Although many fishing families have
been rehoused in the blocks overlooking the harbour, others continue to live on their boats.
A trip through Aberdeen's congested typhoon shelter at night still gives a fascinating
glimpse into the life of Hong Kong's fishing families, much of it played out very publicly on
open deck. Although numbers of professional fishermen are declining, fishing remains an
important industry; 21,600 working fishermen on 4,800 fishing vessels were registered
in 1996. Three quarters of the fish landed in Hong Kong are caught by trawling.
The picture above shows the famous Jumbo Floating Restaurant moored in Shum Wan,
south Aberdeen.

KOWLOON

A Junk

1978

A junk heads straight for the camera, while
I was on a boat in Victoria Harbour. These
beautiful craft looked good from every angle
and perspective.

RIGHT

Central and Kowloon

1998

Taken from the Peak, this shot of Central and
Kowloon shows Exchange Square with the
Outlying Islands Ferry Pier in front of it.
On the left is the new 80 storey
"The Center", the lights of which change
colour every few seconds.

PREVIOUS PAGE

Tsim Sha Tsui Clock Tower

1996 & 1971

This is all that remains of the Kowloon-Canton
Railway Terminal, demolished in 1978.
The clock, installed in 1921, was beset with
technical problems, and even now each of the
four clock faces shows a slightly different time.
Behind is the Hong Kong Cultural Centre
complex, built on the site of the demolished
railway station and opened in 1989. Dubbed
'the ski-slope' by locals, many have wondered
how a building which would certainly provide
those inside with one of the world's finest views
came to be designed without windows.

Lion Dances

1994

Lion dances welcome arriving cruise-ship passengers at Ocean Terminal. These boisterous, energetic dances, accompanied by rhythmic drums, gongs and clashing cymbals, are performed at a wide variety of propitious occasions in Hong Kong - anything from a small hospital fete or the official opening of a major new office block or hotel to a traditional Chinese festival. The Chinese for dancing lions *mo si* sounds similar to the words for 'no trouble', and thus the lions are helpful in securing a troublefree future.

LEFT
Ocean Terminal

1979

The Queen Elizabeth II and the SS Canberra lie alongside Ocean Terminal, the main berth for luxury cruise liners.

Peninsula Hotel

1996

The new extension of the Peninsula Hotel, with the dome of the Space Museum in front. One of the great old hotels of Asia, 'the Pen' opened in December 1928. It was here that the Governor of Hong Kong formally surrendered to the Japanese in 1941, after which it briefly became the Toa Hotel and the headquarters of the Japanese governor. Owners, Hongkong and Shanghai Hotels, restarted the hotel operation in 1946, and have continued to upgrade the property since then to maintain the Pen's position as the grande dame of Hong Kong's hotels. In 1994 the new tower opened and the hotel's room count increased from 210 to 300. Despite the recent appearance of many of the world's top hotel brand names in the territory, none can rival the fame or atmosphere of the Peninsula's gracious, high-ceilinged lobby, for so long one of 'the' places to meet in Asia. At the 1928 opening, an American visitor was heard to say: " I'd feel rich here if I hadn't a dime in my bag." The Sheraton Hotel is on the right and the YMCA, a comfortable hotel which belies the spartan image conjured up by its name, is on the left.

Nathan Road and Mong Kok

2000

The Golden Mile of Nathan Road and its side streets such as Peking Road are ablaze with colour at night. Shops stay open until the early hours. This is understandable when rents in this area reach dizzying heights. A money changer here is paying HK$110,000.00 (£8,800.00) per month for a space of 34.5 square feet! Nathan Road is Kowloon's main thoroughfare, and the heart of Hong Kong's retail life. It was named after Sir Matthew Nathan, Governor from 1904-1907, who had ambitiously hoped to build a road to Guangzhou and beyond. In fact, it never got further than Boundary Street on the edge of Kowloon. It is hard to reconcile a resident's description of the road in the 1920s as 'a lovely peaceful place, lined with large trees' with the present noisy, fumed-filled road thronging with shoppers from every corner of the world. the world. The pictures above are of streets in Mong Kok which is probably one of the most purely Chinese areas in Hong Kong. Cluttered with thousands of colourful signs it is packed with small shops, local restaurants, markets, doctor's surgeries and night clubs. For the more adventurous visitor it is a very rewarding area to explore

120

The man with the golden teeth

1994

This man was doing touch-up paintwork on the hull of the Queen Elizabeth II.
I was sitting in the lounge with the executive chef when his smiling face full of golden dental
work appeared at the window.

Shanghai Street

1986

A traditional herbal teashop on the corner of Shanghai Street and Public Square Street in
Mong Kok. Sadly, this building has been demolished, but the business of selling herbal tea
is still thriving in Hong Kong. The proprietors of this shop are still doing good business in
their newer, grander premises.

Tin Hau Temple, Yau Ma Tei
1996

Buried amongst the anonymous-looking tenement blocks, this temple houses the sea goddess, who is also the Taoist Queen of Heaven. When the temple complex was built over 100 years ago, the sea was a few yards away, but reclamation has pushed the water back several blocks and buildings have cut off any sea view. The temple was carefully restored in the 1970s, keeping as much to the original materials and design as possible. These huge spiral coils of incense hanging from the roof represent a long-term offering, for some will burn for as long as two weeks. For around HK$100 you may have your name hung on to one of the coils.

Tin Hau Temple, Yau Ma Tei

1995

Built between 1870-1876, there are in fact four temples dedicated to a great many gods. There are three shelves with images of the Tai Sui (the 60 gods of the year), one god representing each year of the 60-year cycle. Whatever the problem, the right god to handle the difficulty can be found here. Immediately to the left is the entrance to Shea Tan, dedicated to the local community.

Tung Choi Street Market, Mong Kok

1994

This is the biggest of all Hong Kong street markets. All manner of merchandise can be
found here at very competitive prices, but it is clothes that provide the best bargains.
The other famous market is in Temple Street to the west of Nathan Road.

Wong Tai Sin Temple, Chinese New Year

Worshippers with joss sticks. Built in 1973, this is one of Hong Kong's newest temples, and throughout the year attracts huge numbers who come to give offerings of fruit and other food, burn joss sticks and to pray to the gods. Both young and old from all sections of Hong Kong's community worship here. Of all Hong Kong's gods, the Taoist Wong Tai Sin has the best reputation for granting the wishes of devotees, particularly those related to illness and horse racing tips. The temple is surrounded by fortune tellers and stalls selling temple tack. There are more than 350 Chinese temples in the territory, 43 of which are managed by the Chinese Temples Committee as public temples.

RIGHT
Hungry Ghost Festival

1984

A bustling scene in Kwun Tong where large-scale celebrations for the festival are in full swing. During the festival the vast number of ghosts, or disembodied spirits, that are believed to roam freely at this time of year, need to be placated with gifts and with several nights of operatic shows. The brilliantly coloured matshed theatre in the background is erected specially to house these performances, and is removed at the end of the festival.

Dried-food wholesale store

1996

A dried-food wholesale store in Kowloon City, stocked for Chinese New Year with an impressive array of dried sausages and fish, including abalone, fish skin, shark's fin, shrimps, dried mushrooms and other delicacies. Some of the prices are staggering: abalone, hanging in the centre of the picture, is HK$3,600 a piece (around £280) and a catty (0.67 kg) of birds' nests costs the same.

Village Children

A little girl lovingly tends to her brother. One often sees young children being responsible for their even younger siblings. Above left: This traditional means of carrying a baby is still quite widely used in Hong Kong.

FAR LEFT

Kau Wah Keng

1981

This old tile-roofed village lies nestled between the industrial concrete of Cheung Sha Wan and Lai Chi Kok and the vast container port of Kwai Chung. Amazingly it is still almost intact today, although negotiations are under way with a property developer to demolish it and build a huge residential estate of high rises.

Monkey God Festival

1984

At this festival in Sau Mau Ping a 'medium', empowered for the occasion with the supernatural abilities of the impish Monkey God, demonstrates the Monkey's invulnerability by plunging his feet into boiling oil. In Chinese legends Monkey corresponds to a Puck or Robin Goodfellow in England. He is a naughty character who successfully goes against the establishment whether human or divine.

His exploits were told in a long saga called the "Journey to the West" which described the adventures of the monk, Yuen Tsong, who went to India to fetch the Buddhist scriptures. This was a true story but fostered a huge collection of legendary tales and characters of whom the Monkey is one. He stole the Peaches of Immortality from Heaven and thereby made himself indestructible. In other gory feats at the festival to celebrate his birthday, mediums climb ladders with rungs made of sharp knives, cut their tongues with a sword and bite into porcelain cups and plates, stick sharp razors through their cheeks and run on burning charcoals.

The Kowloon Peninsula

1995

Shot from Fei Ngo Shan (Kowloon Peak). A favourite view for photographs,
not least because it is possible to drive a good way up the mountain with
all the camera equipment. From here the view encompasses Tsz Wan Shan
on the right, the vast housing estates of Choi Hung and Ngau Tau Kok, and
part of Kowloon Bay on the left. The old airport at Kai Tak dominates the
centre of this now historic photograph. The lights went out here for the last
time on 6 July 1998, 73 years after Harry Abbott first flew from there. The
government is still undecided on how to proceed with the redevelopment of
the area. Let's hope that they decide on something visionary, exciting and
inspiring and not yet another apartment/shopping mall complex.

NEW TERRITORIES

Clearwater Bay Golf and Country Club

1996

Clearwater Bay golf course and Clearwater Bay Peninsula, with 344-metre high Junk Peak (Tiu Yue Yung) rising gracefully from the bay. The awe-inspiring 14th hole is set against a backdrop of the South China Sea. If you slice the ball only slightly here, it will meet a watery grave. This wonderfully positioned club is the largest in the territory, covering a site of 145 hectares and boasting an 18-hole course and a second nine-hole golf course, as well as marina club, pool and luxury clubhouse. Established in 1982 amid gloomy predictions for its future, the pessimists have been proved hopelessly wrong; corporate debentures, which could be bought for just HK$75,000 in 1984, are now selling for well over HK$2 million.

PREVIOUS PAGE
North Sai Kung

1995

Three Fathoms Cove (Kei Ling Ha Hoi) with the tiny island of Wu Chau in the centre.

Clearwater Bay Beach
1996

Sunday at Clearwater Bay Beach (Tsing Shui Wan)
on the Sai Kung Peninsula. This area in the eastern
New Territories is one of the most unspoilt and
breathtakingly beautiful in the territory.

Tin Hau Festival

1985

Part of a flotilla of gaily decorated lighters and junks make
their way towards the temple at Joss House Bay on the
23rd day of the 3rd moon.

OVERLEAF

Hung Shing Kung's birthday

1976

An elaborate shrine, or *fa-pau*, constructed of bamboo and
paper, is brought by boat to the festival celebrating Hung
Shing Kung's birthday at Kau Sai Island. A favourite god
amongst Hong Kong's seafarers, Hung Shing Kung is
believed by some followers to be the Dragon King of the
Southern Seas, while others claim he was a Tang Dynasty
official, much admired for his accurate weather forecasts.
But these vague credentials in no way detract from the jovial
annual birthday celebrations held in Hung Shing Kung
temples in several fishing communities throughout
the territory.

Tin Hau Festival

1993

A dancing lion leads the way as a towering floral *fa-pau* is presented for
blessing in front of a matshed temple in Castle Peak, Tuen Mun.

Fish Farms

1996

Fish farms at Tai Wong Kung, Clearwater Bay. Marine fish farming is a
well-established industry around the coast of the eastern New Territories.

RIGHT

Hebe Haven

1984

Diced root vegetables are dried in the sun before being pickled at a farm
in Hebe Haven, Sai Kung.

Mainland junks

1981

This wonderful flotilla of junks from Amoy assembled in Joss House Bay, after sailing south
to escape the threat of an earthquake. Hong Kong police cordoned off the boats for the
several days they remained in the territory, and, since the earthquake on the mainland never
materialized, an aura of mystery has remained around the whole episode.

Live red snapper
1996

Live red snapper, a popular local delicacy for sale in
a wholesale fish market in Castle Peak.

RIGHT
Sai Kung Peninsula
1995

Empty rocky promontories and inlets sheltering
small fishing communities still characterize the
beautiful High Island Reservoir area. This view from
the Sai Kung Man Yee Road, which borders the
reservoir, looks southwest across Rocky Harbour
(Leung Shuen Wan Hoi), with the fishing village of
Sha Kiu Tau in the middle distance, and the
rugged silhouette of Bluff Island (Sha Tong
Hau Shan) behind.

OVERLEAF
Aerial Patterns
1975–96

Detail captions on page 226, the last page.

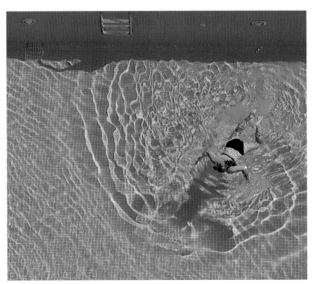

Tai Long Wan

1986

This magnificent aerial view of Tai Long Wan (literally, Big Wave Bay) is one of the very few
Hong Kong vistas which has hardly changed in 26 years. On Sundays the bay becomes full
of pleasure craft and people enjoying the clean water and even occasional surf. Memories
of wonderful tranquil days spent here linger on forever.

Tat Hong Channel

1977

Four junks from the mainland head for China under full sail through this channel which is east of Hong Kong Island. Cape Collinson is in the background.

RIGHT
Inner Port Shelter, Sai Kung

1996

This view of one of Hong Kong's most beautiful areas is from the main dam of High Island, looking towards Sai Kung with Urn Island (Tai Tau Chau) and Kau Sai Chau, now the site of Hong Kong's first public golf couse, on the left. Those lucky enough to hire or own boats weekend overnight in the calm bays along the shore. It was a favourite water skiing place.

OVERLEAF
Sai Kung Peninsula

1995

From Sai Kung Man Yee Road, looking south across the inlet of Pak Lap Tsai to the South China Sea. The road is part of the MacLehose Trail, the 100-km cross-country trail, named after one of Hong Kong's most admired Governors (1971-1982), which leads walkers through some of Hong Kong's most spectacular mountainous terrain.

Tin Hau Temple, Tap Mun Island

1996

Intricate figures of gods, folklore characters and lucky symbols, made in the famous
Shek Wan potteries of South China, are traditional features of Chinese temple roofs.
This particularly impressive line-up tops off the Tin Hau Temple on Tap Mun Chau, the small,
peaceful island that lies at the convergence of Tolo and Long Harbours in the northeast of
the territory. The temple is one of the most beautiful and best preserved of Hong Kong's
many temples dedicated to the sea goddess and Queen of Heaven, Tin Hau. The richly
ornamented statue of her (right) is the focal point inside.

Tap Mun Island Ta Chiu Festival

1999

I was privileged to be invited by Loi Lam, one of the elders of this remote island village on Mirs Bay, to attend the third day of their most important festival, which only occurs once every 10 years. Relatives and guests from all over the world come to participate in it. The highlight of the festival is the removal of the Gods from the temple and their carriage on a flotilla of emblazoned fishing boats off to a neighbouring island and then back safely to their original home. This lasts about 3 hours and is highlighted by exploding firecrackers, lion dancers and the clashing of cymbals and gongs. This year the entertainment was supplied by a marvelous Mainland puppet troupe as well as the traditional full scale Chinese opera.

Yim Tin Tsai fish farm

1994

The view looks south across Tolo Harbour with the Chinese University on the hillside in the distance. Many of the more accessible villages in this area have become dormitory towns, but here people still earn a living from farming and fishing, On the right, fish on sale in markets in the New Territories. Cantonese fish dishes depend on the freshest of ingredients and ideally the fish must be live when bought. With expert timing, and masterful understanding of natural flavours, they are typically steamed in a sauce of oil, fresh ginger and green onions, or lightly stir-fried, to create possibly the world's greatest seafood cuisine.

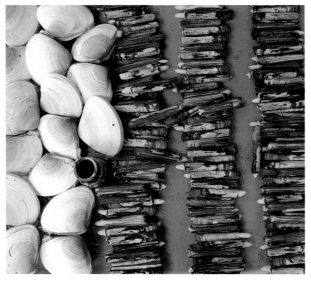

Sha Tin

1971 & 1995

In 1971, Sha Tin was a fishing town, its harbour dotted
with small leisure boats, and providing anchorage for
a floating restaurant. Now, as a result of a major
government-led scheme to build a network of new
towns in the New Territories, the harbour has been
filled in and half a million people live in this massive
satellite town. By 1998, 700,000 people will live
there - over half of them in public housing. The new
Sha Tin, photographed from the air in 1995, has many
of the trappings of an independent town, with
shopping centres, schools, a famous racecourse with
Penfold Park in the centre, museum, concert hall and
university. The old floating restaurant has been
'anchored' to the reclaimed land.

Ladies' Day at Sha Tin Racecourse
1996

71,200 people turned up on November 16 to watch nine races in each of which lady jockeys were competing. They spent HK$1.326 billion (£106,000,000) betting on these nine races. This phenomenal sum easily exceeds the turnover of any other racecourse in the world. The feature race was the Ladies' Purse, first run in 1863. Traditionally, gold sovereigns were presented to the winning parties by an unmarried daughter of one of Hong Kong's dignitaries but since 1990, lunar year gold coins have replaced them. The racecourse was opened in 1978. It is equipped with every conceivable modern luxury including piped music in the stables and heated swimming pools for the horses. It has the world's biggest trackside video matrix which provides slow motion film and instant replays of the races, as well as all the information of the betting and odds in two languages. The 250 acres of reclaimed land accommodates three tracks, stands for 83,000 racegoers and a central public park.

Sai Kung

1989

An old lady tending cows near the village of Ko Tung Ha Yeung in Sai Kung.

BOTTOM LEFT
Ta Kwu Ling

1996

A farmhand from mainland China at work in the closed area of Ta Kwu Ling along the Chinese border.

FAR LEFT
Tai Po Kau

1971

Gathering seaweed by the roadside at Tai Po Kau. The shallow waters in this picture have gone, engulfed by a massive reclamation project which provided land for the new town of Tai Po, now home to 258,000 people.

Sha Lo Tung Valley

1989 & 1993

A left-over from another era, the traditional Hakka village of Cheung
Uk lies in the unspoilt Sha Lo Tung Valley, a few miles northeast of
the Tai Po Road. Twenty years ago Cheung Uk had 450 inhabitants;
now the population has dwindled to a few old ladies who tend the
ancestral hall. The valley itself, enclosed on all sides so that it is
invisible below, is home to a rich variety of flora and fauna, and its
meandering stream is the only unpolluted, slow-flowing stream in
the entire territory. But the valley's future is uncertain; a long drawn-
out battle between conservationists and former residents who would
like to develop the site into a luxury residential estate and golf
course is still to be resolved.

Old lady of Tsuen Wan

1980

Hong Kong's old people have not always been well catered for in fast changing Hong Kong, but this old lady was living in a special home where she could retain some of her self-sufficiency through the support of the Buddhist nuns of Chuk Lam Monastery, near Tsuen Wan.

FAR LEFT

Temple at Nam Chung

1989

This is one of my favourite photographs as it was a lovely surprise to find this little temple in an isolated place and in such wonderful light. The temple is located near Starling Inlet (Sha Tau Kok Hoi). I have since returned and it has been cleaned up and painted which has sadly destroyed all the atmosphere seen in the old photograph.

Luk Keng duck farm

1992

A duck farm in an idyllic setting near Starling Inlet (Sha Tau Kok Hoi). Like other traditional
forms of farming in Hong Kong, duck production is declining, and much of the excellent
duck consumed in Hong Kong's restaurants is now imported.

FAR RIGHT
Sheung Shui

1977

A small boy catches up on his homework while waiting for his school bus near the village. The Chinese characters translate as "The Bridge for the Convenience of my Mother". It was built in 1710 by Tang Chuen Yuen to enable his mother to visit her grandchildren across the stream.

FAR BOTTOM RIGHT
Man Shek Tong, Sheung Shui

1977

This is the main ancestral hall of the Lui Clan. It is a three hall type building and believed to date from 1751. It has the richest wood carvings of ancestral halls in the territory and has recently been totally renovated. At this time it housed a temporary primary school, which has long since moved to new premises. Twenty-five years ago there were barely enough school places in Hong Kong to allow every child a primary education. Educational opportunities have improved dramatically at all levels, and now a quarter of school leavers go on to tertiary education in the territory.

Chinese New Year Harvest

1996

The delicate peach blossoms are the most sought-after decorative and auspicious plants at Chinese New Year; peachwood is viewed as a potent enemy of demons and the peach itself is an emblem of longevity. It is vital the flowers open just at the right moment and girls from across the border are employed in the weeks before the New Year festival to pick off any blossoms that might flower too early. The orange trees are also auspicious at New Year as the Chinese name for them is "Gat" which means "Good Fortune". They produce bitter kumquats, but the dried skin is used as a condiment in many dishes or as confectionery.

ABOVE, LEFT & LEFT INSIDE GATEFOLD
The Hui Yuen Tree (Wishing Tree) at Lam Tsuen

2001

The Hui Yuen Tree legend is recent. A boat dweller, sick for a long time, seemed incurable until he prayed in front of a tree in Lam Tsuen, near Tai Po, and recovered completely. News spread and people began to believe that these were enchanted trees which could make wishes come true. It is now a very popular place to visit on the Ist & 15th day of every Moon of the Lunar calendar, but especially within the Spring Festival and at Chinese New Year, when these pictures were taken. After visiting the Tin Hau Temple nearby people pay homage to the trees and make wishes, which involves writing names, wishes and other information on a "Ng Bo Dip" or paper mascot attached to an orange with string and throwing it up into the tree until it catches in as high a branch as possible.

Chinese New Year

2001

Falling in late January or early February this is the most widely observed festival. Each year is named after one of 12 animals, all having different characteristics. Legend tells how Lord Buddha called all earth's animals to him but only 12 obeyed. To reward them a year was given to each. The New Year heralds a period of goodwill, the settling of debts & quarrels and visits to temples, fortune tellers and close relatives. New clothes are bought along with flowers, peach blossoms and orange trees. Special foods are prepared, often vegetarian; red Lai-see packets full of money given to children and unmarried relatives and everywhere one is greeted with the words "Kung Hei Fat Choi" ("Best wishes and prosperity"). Thousands use the 3 day holiday to return to China. The ceiling above and most of the pictures on the left are of the beautiful Kwun Yum temple in Tai Hang, which is a very popular shrine at this time.

Lau Fau Shan, Deep Bay

1975

A farmer has commandeered the services of all his family, down to the very youngest,
to help prepare the radish (*law bak*) crop for the markets of Kowloon.

RIGHT
Green Organic Farm

1995

The 'Produce Green Organic Farm' near Loi Tung was established by a foundation to help
preserve traditional, chemical-free, methods of farming. Part of the land is farmed by
enthusiasts, and the rest is leased to full-time farmers who raise produce to sell to the 35,000
visitors who pass through each year. The rice paddy here is almost the last in the territory.

Ha Tsuen Ta Chiu Festival

1976

Elders waiting to greet VIP visitors at the festival. This large-scale Taoist festival, held just once every ten years in the village of Ha Tsuen near Yuen Long, ambitiously aims to wipe out evil in the whole area, restore peace, and renew life for the entire population. The event is so important that emigrants return to Hong Kong especially to participate in this festival which can last up to a week. The Taoist priests are reading the names of all member villagers from the long scroll. These festivals are held all over the New Territories. At Lam Tsuen in 1981, 23 villages took part, the matshed theatre held 3,000 people, more than a thousand came back from Europe and the name list totalled nearly 7,000.

OUTLYING ISLANDS

Lamma Island
1980

A lone junk makes its way past Lamma Island, with the islands of the South China Sea in the distance. The preceding page shows the island from a helicopter hovering near Yung Shue Bay; the craggy ribbon of island stretching away to the northeast. In the distance on Hong Kong Island, across the busy shipping lanes of the Lamma Channel, can be seen the highrises of Western, Pokfulam and Aberdeen. Lamma is the third largest island in the territory, after Lantau and Hong Kong, but has largely escaped development; no roads link the small pockets of habitation where some 8,000 people live.

RIGHT
Fat Tong Mun
1975

On a rare becalmed sea, a junk is oared through Fat Tong Mun, the narrow channel of water between the island of Tung Lung Chau and the Clearwater Bay Peninsula. One of the most attractive features of these wonderful butterflies of the sea were the sails - invariably patched in different colours or full of holes - yet still able to propel the craft long distances.

Hei Ling Chau

1973

Fishing over, the nets gathered and sails furled, the children are left to do acrobatics in the rigging. In the background is Hei Ling Chau, a small island off Lantau.

LEFT

Silvermine Bay, Lantau

1996

Two ferries leave Silvermine Bay (Ngan Kwong Wan) on Lantau Island. In the distance is Hong Kong Island, with Victoria Peak and the buildings of Western and Pokfulam clearly visible. On the left in the middle distance, is the smaller island of Peng Chau, a port of call for ferries en route from Lantau to Central.

Lantau Island

1973

Farmers could still be seen tilling the soil with a wooden plough drawn by
a buffalo in the 1970s. This farm and village, now totally abandoned, was at
Ha Keng on the Chi Ma Wan Peninsula.

Lantau Link, Kap Shui Mun Bridge

1998

Part of the 34 km direct road and rail network leading to Hong Kong
International Airport at Chek Lap Kok. Ma Wan Island is in the centre and
Ting Kau Bridge, which marks the beginning of the new Route 3 Toll Road
through Tai Lam Tunnel on to Yuen Long, is on the far left.

Chek Lap Kok Terminal

1998

Only 9 years from start to finish, but costing US$20 Billion, Hong Kong's new airport was the largest infrastructure project ever undertaken globally. Designed by Sir Norman Foster, the terminal building is the biggest covered structure in the world.

LEFT

Silvermine Bay, Lantau

1995

A short walk from the ferry is this relic of the past, probably part of an old fortified village.

Po Lin Monastery, Lantau

1995

The world's largest seated, outdoor, bronze Buddha dominates
the dramatic mountainous landscape above the monastery.
Completed in 1993, it took six years, and HK$70 million, to create
this 26.4 metre-high bronze. The statue weighs 202 tonnes, and sits
on a lotus throne on top of a three-platformed altar, with 268 steps
leading up to it. The monks at Po Lin designed the Buddha, but
they had help in construction from mainland Chinese engineers.
The lights which illuminate the Buddha so spectacularly are only
turned on once or twice a month on auspicious days because the
electricity costs are so high. The small temple of Wei To on the right
acts as an entrance gate to the monastery.

Po Lin Monastery

1996

The Giant Buddha, and interiors at the
Po Lin Monastery, Lantau Island. Po Lin means
"Precious Lotus", the lotus flower being the symbol
of the Buddhist faith. The affluent monastery
complex is relatively new; most of it has been built
since 1970, although the first three monks took up
residence in a few stone huts on this site in 1905.
Today the monastery is a large and thriving
community with thousands of visitors arriving each
day to see the Buddha. Inside the ornate two-storey
main temple, which is dedicated to the Three
Precious Buddhas, are clusters of tasselled lanterns
hung from the richly carved and painted arched
roof, gilded shrines, and long hangings of red and
yellow embroidery. The large brass bell, cast in
1965, is engraved with the names of the donors
in red characters.

Kwun Yum Temple, Lantau

1995

Kwun Yum, the Buddhist Goddess of Mercy, is loved by both Taoists and Buddhists, and many temples are dedicated to her in Hong Kong. But this one, painstakingly restored in 1995 with no expense spared by a wealthy Hong Kong businessman, is one of the most beautiful. Craftsmen were brought from China to ensure that every detail of the building was of the highest quality. The original site was granted by Sir Cecil Clementi (Governor of Hong Kong 1925-1930) to his favourite amah, who built a small temple here.

Tai O, Lantau

1995

An anachronistic rope-drawn ferry used to connect the two sides of the village divided by a creek. The sampan which ferried passengers across the narrow creek cost 50 cents a crossing and survived until late 1996 when it was superseded by a cement bridge.

Tai O, Lantau

1995

The village, on the western tip of Lantau, is a strongly traditional fishing
community, where ramshackle houses on stilts spill out over the creek.
The family are watching the dragon boat racing. The row of pot plants adds
a charming homely touch to the balcony of this precarious-looking dwelling.

Dragon Boat Races in Tai O, Lantau

1995

Hundreds of fire crackers explode to mark the start of the races, with a noise so deafening, it must leave those standing nearby unable to hear properly for weeks to come. Fire crackers have been banned in Hong Kong since the 1967 riots when gun powder normally used for these small explosions was diverted for use in bombs. Nonetheless, they can still be seen - or heard - on festive occasions in remote corners of the territory. Tai O has always been a fishing village but before 1841 it was notorious as a pirate haven.

Tai O
1995

Wearing the flat-crowned Tanka hat favoured by many of Hong Kong's fishing community, a woman sorts through a basket of dried shrimps. Tai O reputedly has the finest quality salt-dried fish in Hong Kong.

RIGHT
Salt-dried fish
1995

A typical array of salt-dried fish found in shops through-out the territory.

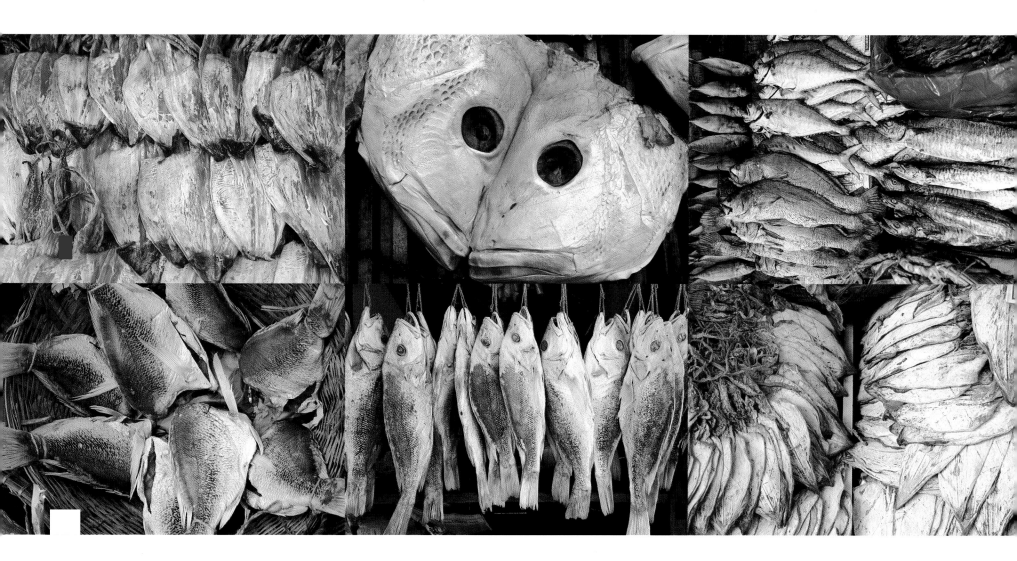

Tai O

1994

The sun sets behind fishing boats at anchor in Tai O, the heart of Lantau's fishing industry.

RIGHT
Pui O

1978

Hong Kong's glorious patchwork landscape of rice paddies has virtually disappeared.
Vegetable growing is much more profitable and the amount of land devoted to rice had
dropped from over 9,000 hectares in 1954 to less than 10 hectares by the end of the 1980s.

Tanka family, Tap Mun

1986

The Tanka were said to be exiled to the sea for plotting against a Sung Dynasty emperor who decreed that their descendants should never again live on land. Families lived, gave birth and died in their tiny sampans and old junks.

LEFT
Hei Ling Chau

1973

This remains one of my all-time favourite photographs. It was taken on a balmy May evening during a boat picnic to Lantau. The sun is setting over Sunset Peak and the fishing family are on their last catch of the day,

Cheung Chau

1984

Fishing boats at anchor on this small, densely populated island, with an area of just
2.3 square kilometres, to the southwest of Hong Kong Island. Traditionally its people have
focused on fishing, with a little piracy and smuggling on the side, but increasingly
commuters who work in Hong Kong have set up home here.

LEFT

Cheung Chau Bun Festival

1976

The small Taoist shrine, erected especially for the festival, is constructed out of hanging
fabrics and paintings depicting deities and revered historical characters. Its guardian is
taking a smoking break - probably one of the last generation in Hong Kong to use
traditional bamboo pipes.

Cheung Chau Bun Festival

1980s

The six-day festival is celebrated in May with a unique procession. Three vast wooden towers, each covered with some 5,000 white buns stamped with a goodwill message, are erected near the Pak Tai Temple. Their purpose is to appease the hungry spirits of pirate victims, whose mutilated bodies were found in the 1880s on the island. The festival also gives thanks to Pak Tai, Emperor of the North and God of the Sea, for protecting the islanders since the 1770s from various plagues. The festivities include Chinese opera, lion dances, stilt dances and a fabulous procession, featuring many legendary figures as well as more contemporary celebrities.

OVERLEAF
The Float Procession

1980s

The young children held aloft in Cheung Chau's famous street processions are always the stars of the island's Bun Festival. Aged between five and eight, they are supported on frames and carried shoulder-high throughout the whole parade to create an elaborate, often whimsical, tableau representing characters in history or mythology. Decked out in thick makeup, with heavy costumes and headgear, the children have to spend some four hours, motionless, in the baking sun - small wonder their faces are not always ecstatic.

Cheung Chau Bun Festival

1974

The traditional climax of the six-day festival used to be a midnight scramble up 20-metre
towers of buns. The three huge conical bamboo and paper towers, covered from top to
bottom in layers of pink and white buns, are pictured. The buns - part of a grand offering to
the ghosts which the festival is attempting to appease - are a symbol of good fortune and a
talisman against sickness for whoever manages to grab one. The higher the bun, the greater
the luck it was supposed to bring. In the mad dash up the towers by the young men at the
festival, it took just a few minutes to strip them bare of buns. The practice was banned
officially after one of the towers collapsed in the assault, even though no-one was hurt.
Nowadays the buns are distributed to orderly queues the next morning.

INDEX

Aberdeen 50-51,100-109,154,196,197
Bank of America Building 34-35
Bank of China Building *gatefold* 12,18,28, 39,48,53,60
Bank of China Building (old) 49,56
Bluff Island 152-153
Caldbeck Macgregor 31
Cape Collinson 158
Castle Peak 145,152
Causeway Bay 6-7,73,74,80-81
Central 2-3,6-7,*gatefold* 12-13,18,28,43, 52-53,54,62-63,66,113
Central Plaza *gatefold* 11,74-75
Chek Lap Kok 22,34-35,40,203,205
Cheung Chau 191,222-229
Cheung Chau Bun Festival 224-229
Cheung Kong Centre *gatefold* 12,18,39,53,54,60
Cheung Uk 176-177
Chi Ma Wan Peninsula 196
Chinese New Year 103,106,109,128, 184-185,*gatefold* 186-191
Chinese Opera 69,70-71,164
Chinese University 166
Choi Hung 136-137
Chuk Lam Monastery 179
Citibank Tower 61
Citic Building 11
Clock Tower 52,111
Clearwater Bay 142-143,148,199
Clearwater Bay Golf and Country Club 140-141
Connaught Centre 37,43
Convention and Exhibition Centre 6-7,39,74-75
Cosco Building 13,113
Cumming, Constance Gordon 30
Deep Water Bay 97,98,99
Douglas Castle 59
Dragon boat races 104,105,213-215
Dragon Dance 1,4-5
East Island Corridor 6-7
Eastern Street 55
Exchange Square 18,52,53,113
Fat Tong Mun 193
Fei Ngo Shan (view from) 136-137
Festivals *gatefold* 8,9,10
Foster, Lord Norman 23,60,205
Gammon House 34-35
Giant Buddha 206-209
Glenealy 30
Goldman Sachs 60
Government House 32-33

Green Organic Farm 193
Ha Tsuen Ta Chiu Festival 194,195
Happy Valley 44,45
Headland Road 16-17,60-61
Hebe Haven 149
Hei Ling Chau 28-29,201,220-221
Hongkong and Shanghai Bank 52,53,57,60
Hongkong and Shanghai Bank (old) 32-33, 49,56
Hong Kong Club (old) 48,56
Hong Kong Cricket Club (old) 32-33,43,48, 49,56
Hong Kong Cultural Centre Complex 110
Hong Kong Hilton Hotel 34-35,66
Hong Kong Jockey Club 14-15,170-173
Hui Yuen Tree *gatefold* 186-189,
Hung Shing Kung Festival 146-147
Hungry Ghost Festival 129
I.M.Pei 55,60
Jardine House 43,52
Jean Wong's Ballet School 65,72
Johnston Road 77
Joss House Bay 150,151
Jumbo Floating Restaurant 108
Junk Peak 140
Junks 22,24,38,112,150,151,154,158,198, 199,201
Kai Tak airport 47,136-137
Kam Wa Street market 83
Kap Shui Mun Bridge 203
Kat O Hoi 25
Kau Sai Island 146,147,159
Kau Wah Keng village 132
Kennedy Town *gatefold* 13,54
Kowloon 2-3,110,113,137
Kowloon-Canton Railway Terminal 24,111
Kowloon City 47,130-131
Kwun Yum 94
Kwun Yum Temple(s) *gatefold* 190,191,210-211
Kwun Tong 129
Lai Chi Wo 25
Lamma 16-17,38,90,196-198
Lantau 200-219,230-231
Lantau Link 34-35,203
Lau Fau Shan 192
Lido complex, Repulse Bay 93,94,95
Lippo Centre 61
Lion Dances 115,145,*gatefold* 186-188
Lockhart Road 77
Luk Keng duck farm 180,181
MacLehose Trail 160-161

Mandarin Hotel 32-33,52,57
Man Shek Tong 183
Matilda Hospital (view from) 50-51,107, 230-231
Middle Island 98-99
Mong Kok 118,121,126,127
Monkey God Festival 134,135
Moon (Mid-Autumn) Festival 76
Mount Butler (view from) 80
Mount Gough 43
Mount Kellett (view from) 50-51,230-231
Mount Nicholson 43
Nam Chung Temple 178
Nathan Road 119
Ngau Tau Kok 136,137
Ocean Park 16-17,155
Ocean Terminal *gatefold* 11,68,114,115
Pacific Place 28,66
Peak (view from) 2-3,60-61,113
Peak Tower 52
Peng Chau 200-201
Peninsula Hotel 24,116,117
Po Lin Monastery 206-209
Pok Fu Lam 59,196
Pollock's Path 34-35
Port Shelter 159
Post Office (old) 58
Pui O 219
Princes Building 49
Queen Elizabeth II 114,120
Red Hill 89
Repulse Bay 50,51,92-96
Repulse Bay Hotel 96
Repulse Bay Road 98-99
Rocky Harbour 152-153
Royal Hong Kong Yacht Club 6-7,67
Sai Kung 138-142,152-153,160-161,175
Sau Mau Ping 134-135
Scaffolders 26-27
Sha Kiu Tau village 152-153
Sha Tin 167,168
Sha Tin Races 14-15,169,170-173
Sha Lo Tung Valley 176,177
Shanghai Street 121
Shau Kei Wan 82,83
Shek O Golf Club 87
Shek O Headland 86
Sheraton Hotel 24,116
Sheung Shui 182,183
Shouson Hill 50-51
Shum Wan 50-51,108

Silvermine Bay 200-201,204
Sir Cecil Clementi 81,210
Sir Cecil's Ride 80-81
South Bay 90-91
SS Canberra 114
Standard Chartered Bank (old) 56
Stanley 88,107 & Market 89
Star Cruise *gatefold* 11
Star Ferry 21,52,155
Starling Inlet 178,180
Sunset Peak 220-221,230-231
Supreme Court Building 56-57
Ta Chiu Festival 164-165,194-195
Ta Kwu Ling 85,175
Tai Chi 48
Tai Long Wan 156,157
Tai O 212-218
Tai Po Kau 174
Tai Wong Kung 148
Tai Yuen Street market 46
Tam Kung Festival 107
Tap Mun Island 42,162-165,221
Tat Hong Channel 86,158
The Center 2-3,6-7,*gatefold* 12,18,53,54,113
The Gateway *gatefold* 11
Three Fathoms Cove 138-139
Tiger Balm Gardens 81
Tin Hau 122,123,124,125,144,145,
Tin Hau Temple, Lam Tsuen *gatefold* 186-189
Ting Kau Bridge 203
Tolo Harbour 166
Trams 78-79
Tsim Sha Tsui 2-3,113,119
Tsing Ma Bridge 34-35,40-41
Tsz Wan Shan 136-137
Tung Choi Street 127
Tung Lung Island 86,199
University Hall 59
Victoria Harbour 2-3,*gatefold* 11-13,32-37, 43,63-64
Wanchai 2-3,27,84-85
Wanchai Market 84
Waterfront apartments *gatefold* 11-13
Western harbour 69
Wishing Tree *gatefold* 186-189
Wong Chuk Hang 50-51
Wong Tai Sin Temple 128, *gatefold* 188,190
Yau Ma Tei 36-37,122-125
Yim Tin Tsai fish farms 166
YMCA 24,52
Yung Shue Bay 196-197

PREVIOUS PAGE

Sunset over Lantau Island

2000

Taken from the Matilda Hospital on Mount Kellet this dramatic view takes in the shoreline of Pokfulam on Hong Kong Island in the foreground and almost all of Lantau Island in the distance. Lantau is twice the size of Hong Kong but has little industrial and residential development, although the new airport at Chek Lap Kok threatens this peace and tranquility and sadly it will not be long before the whole island is developed.

TECHNICAL BACKGROUND

Almost all of the photographs taken after 1991 are on Fujichrome Velvia. Prior to this I used Kodachrome for most of the 35mm photographs and Ektachrome or Agfachrome for the larger formats. The reason for the switch to Velvia was principally because it was the first film to match and surpass the vivid colours and saturation of Kodachrome, but also because it could be processed and back in one's hands within two hours. Kodachrome had to be sent to Australia and two weeks would pass before the results came back.

The problem with Velvia, as with Kodachrome, is the slow speed. As I used to do a lot of aerial photography from vibrating helicopters with polarising filters which cut the speed by a further 60%, this meant I needed a very firm and steady hand. Many photographs would be ruined by minute camera shake. However, there have been no other films which can match the brilliant, intense colours combined with superb sharpness of these two films.

The photographs of the fishermen on page 28-29 and page 214-215 would not have been possible on colour transparency films such as Kodachrome or Velvia. These were shot on colour negative film, which has a much greater latitude, and I was therefore able to expose for the shadows and faces of the fishermen and prevent the background from washing out which would have happened on transparency or diapositive film.

Hong Kong is a photographer's heaven in that it is full of light and colour, but it is not always an easy place to photograph. The weather is often unconducive to photography as there are very few times of the year when the air is clear. Even back in the 1970s you had to pick your days very carefully. On many occasions, laden down with camera equipment, I have trekked across to the Peak on a clear fine day, only to find that within minutes grey black clouds appeared from nowhere. Now that I am living in London and visit Hong Kong sporadically these problems become even more acute.

The photography of people has never been easy in Hong Kong. In earlier days one was constantly abused and almost attacked if one pointed a camera at people, particularly simple folk living in country areas and on the outlying islands. The old suspicion that a photograph or camera robbed the subject of its soul was still strongly entrenched when I started photographing Hong Kong. Despite these minor problems Hong Kong has been a very rewarding and exciting place to record, with its continual changes and developments and its wonderful situation next to the sea.

Captions for pages 154 & 155
Aerial Patterns

1. 1988. Aberdeen: fishing boats at anchor.
2. 1975. Paddy field and old village, Yuen Long.
3. 1986. Fish Farm, near Tap Mun Island, Long Harbour.
4. 1994. Previously "Air House", it was the first private residence to be sold for $1 million and is now worth hundreds of millions.
5. 1980. A junk, the butterfly of the China Seas.
6. 1986. The Mai Po Marshes, near Yuen Long, famous for their bird population.
7. 1995. Shenzhen in China, across the river. The duck and fish farms are in Hong Kong.
8. 1996. A pool in Repulse Bay.
9. 1994. The New Territories is rapidly becoming a container park. This is near Tuen Mun.
10. 1993. Rollercoaster at Ocean Park which first opened in 1977 and has had more than 37 million visitors since then.
11. 1985. The New Territories. Farms near Fanling.
12. 1993. The Middle Kingdom, Ocean Park, a Chinese cultural village that recreates 5,000 years of Chinese history.
13. 1994. Repulse Bay Beach on a Saturday.
14. 1994. A Star Ferry. The Star Ferry Company was founded in 1897 by a Parsee, Dorabjee Nowrojee, who arrived a cook and ended up the prosperous owner of King Edward Hotel, reputedly the best in town. 96,000 people still cross the harbour by Star Ferry every day. There are 12 ferries in operation.
15. 1994. The Typhoon Shelter at Sham Wan, Aberdeen.
16. 1988. Port Shelter and Rocky Harbour, Sai Kung.
17. 1979. The boat building yards at Shum Wan, Aberdeen.
18. 1993. Fairview Gardens, Yuen Long, New Territories.

Hong Kong SAR

N ↑

Scale 1: 200 000

0	2	4	6	8	10 kms

0	2	4	6 miles

CHINA

She

Deep Bay

Lok
Ch

*Mai Po
Marshes*

Lau Fau
Shan

Nam Sang
Wai

58

Tin Shui
Wai

Yuen
Long

Kam Tin

**NEW
TERRITOR**

Tuen
Mun

*Tai Lam
Chung
Reservoir*

▲
Castle

▲
507

*Peak
583*

Tir
B

Ma Wan

Legend

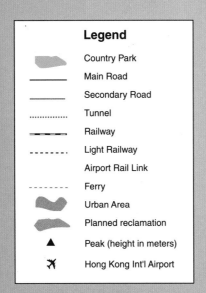	Country Park
	Main Road
	Secondary Road
....	Tunnel
	Railway
- - - - -	Light Railway
	Airport Rail Link
- - - - -	Ferry
	Urban Area
	Planned reclamation
▲	Peak (height in meters)
✈	Hong Kong Int'l Airport

Urmston Road

The Brothers

*Tsing Ma
Bridge*

*Kap Shui
Mun Bridge*

Tsing

✈
Hong Kong
International Airport

**Discovery
Bay**

Peng Chau

Kau Y
Chau

Tung
Chung

Lantau

Island

Mui Wo

Silvermine Bay

Sunshine
Island

Tai O

Po Lin ●
Monastery

*Lantau
Peak*

▲
933

▲ *Sunset*
869

Peak

Hei Ling
Chau

West Lamma Channel

Yu

Fan Lau

Cheung
Chau

Lantau Channel

Shek Kwu
Chau

Soko Islands